MW00991014

Alexander Gresbek

Neil Diamond - From Brooklyn To Broadway

© 2023

Introduction

Neil Diamond is a prominent American singer-songwriter, born on January 24, 1941. He has established himself as one of the best-selling musicians of all time, having sold over 130 million records worldwide. Diamond's music has touched the hearts of millions and his ten No. 1 singles on the U.S. Billboard Hot 100 and Adult Contemporary charts are proof of his success.

Diamond's early career was marked by his songwriting ability. He wrote songs for several well-known artists, including The Monkees, Elvis Presley, and Cliff Richard. However, his true talent as a singer and songwriter began to shine in the late 1960s and 1970s, with a string of hit songs that have become classics.

Some of Diamond's most popular songs include "Cracklin' Rosie", "Song Sung Blue", "Longfellow Serenade", "I've Been This Way Before", "If You Know What I Mean", "Desirée", "You Don't Bring Me Flowers", "America", "Yesterday's Songs", and "Heartlight". "Sweet Caroline" is one of his most beloved songs and has become an anthem for sports teams across the United States. Diamond's ability to connect with his audience through his music has earned him numerous accolades. He was inducted into the Songwriters Hall of Fame in 1984, recognizing his contribution to the music industry. In 2011, he was inducted into the Rock and Roll Hall of Fame, cementing his place in music history.

Diamond's talent extends beyond music. He has also acted in films, making his screen debut in the 1980 musical drama film The Jazz Singer. His acting skills were recognized by the Academy of Motion Picture Arts and Sciences, who nominated him for a Golden Globe Award for his performance in the movie.

Throughout his career, Diamond has remained humble and dedicated to his craft. He has continued to write and perform music that resonates with his fans, and his contributions to the music industry have been recognized with the Sammy Cahn Lifetime Achievement Award in 2000 and the Grammy Lifetime Achievement Award in 2018.

In 2011, Diamond was also an honoree at the Kennedy Center Honors, where his contributions to American culture were celebrated. His music has been a source of inspiration for many generations and will continue to be enjoyed for years to come.

In conclusion, Neil Diamond's talent and contribution to the music industry cannot be overstated. He has left an indelible mark on the music world with his heartfelt lyrics, catchy tunes, and soulful performances.

His place in music history is well-deserved, and his influence on generations of musicians and fans is undeniable.

Contents

Part1: His Life and Music

A Boy From Brooklyn

Neil Leslie Diamond was born on January 24, 1941, in Brooklyn, New York City, to a Jewish family. All four of his grandparents were immigrants, from Poland on his father's side and Russia on his mother's. His parents were Rose and Akeeba "Kieve" Diamond, a dry-goods merchant.

Growing up, Neil Diamond lived in several homes in Brooklyn and spent four years in Cheyenne, Wyoming, where his father was stationed in the army. He attended Erasmus Hall High School, where he was a member of the Freshman Chorus and Choral Club, along with classmate Barbra Streisand. However, they were not close friends at the time, as Diamond recalled, "We were two poor kids in Brooklyn.

We hung out in the front of Erasmus High and smoked cigarettes." Also in their class was chess grandmaster Bobby Fischer.

After his family moved to Brighton Beach, Neil Diamond attended Abraham Lincoln High School and was a member of the fencing team. Also on the team was his best friend, future Olympic fencer Herb Cohen. It was during his 16th birthday that he received his first guitar, which would change his life forever.

One summer, when Diamond was still in high school, he spent several weeks at Surprise Lake Camp, a camp for Jewish children in upstate New York, where folk singer Pete Seeger performed a small concert. Watching other children sing songs they wrote themselves had an immediate effect on Diamond, who then became aware of the possibility of writing his own songs.
He said, "And the next thing, I got a guitar when we got back to Brooklyn, started to take lessons and almost immediately began to write songs." His attraction to songwriting was the "first real interest" he had growing up, and it helped him release his youthful "frustrations."
Diamond also used his newly developed skill to write poetry. By writing poems for girls he was attracted to in school, he soon learned it often won their hearts.
His male classmates took note and began asking him to write poems for them, which they would sing and use with equal success.
He spent the summer following his graduation as a waiter in the Catskills resort area, where he first met Jaye Posner, who would years later become

his first wife.

After high school, Diamond attended New York University as a pre-med major on a fencing scholarship, again on the fencing team with Herb Cohen. He was a member of the 1960 NCAA men's championship fencing team. However, he found writing song lyrics more to his liking than attending classes, so he began cutting classes and taking the train up to Tin Pan Alley, where he tried to get some of his songs heard by local music publishers.

In his senior year, when he was just 10 units short of graduation, Sunbeam Music Publishing offered him a 16-week job writing songs for $50 a week. He dropped out of college to accept it, and the rest, as they say, is history.

Neil Diamond's early life was filled with music, poetry, and fencing. He was a gifted songwriter and poet from a young age, and he used his talents to win the hearts of those around him. Although he started out as a pre-med student, his passion for music eventually led him to drop out of college and pursue his dreams of becoming a musician. It was a decision that would change his life forever and launch him to worldwide fame.

Struggling For Success

In the early 1960s, Diamond was working as a songwriter for Sunbeam Music in New York City. However, after just 16 weeks, he was not rehired, and he began writing and singing his own songs for demos.

Diamond did not choose songwriting; it simply absorbed him and became more and more important in his life. He recorded his first unsuccessful singles as "Neil and Jack", a duet with his high school friend Jack Packer. Despite the lack of commercial success, both Cashbox and Billboard magazines gave all four sides positive reviews, and Diamond signed with Columbia Records as a solo performer later in 1962.

Unfortunately, his solo career did not take off, and he was dropped by Columbia Records after only one year. Diamond spent the next seven years writing songs in and out of publishing houses. He wrote wherever he could, including on buses, and used an upright piano above the Birdland Club in New York City. His songs' wordiness was one of the causes of his early nomadic life as a songwriter. He was able to sell only about one song a week during those years, barely enough to survive. Neil often speaks effusively about his years in 'Tin Pan Alley'.

"Everybody wanted one of those geniuses, you had Carole King and Gerry Goffin, Phil Spector, Jerry Lieber, and Mike Stoller, Doc Pomus and Mort Shuman, Barry Mann and Cynthia Weil, Jeff Barry and Ellie Greenwich, Burt Bacharach and Hal David. These people were the geniuses, and everyone wanted to be like them and write as well as them. Together they probably had more of an effect on American contemporary music than anybody."

He found himself only earning enough to spend 35 cents a day on food, but the privacy that he had above the Birdland Club allowed him to focus on writing without distractions. "Something new began to happen. I wasn't under the gun, and suddenly interesting songs began to happen, songs that had things none of the others did."

During this period, Neil Diamond developed a fresh and distinctive sound, which, along with his attractive appearance, positioned him for success. Jeff Barry introduced Neil to Jerry Wexler from

Atlantic Records, who was impressed with Neil's audition and promptly offered him a recording contract. The following day, Neil was assigned to a new label called Bang Records, which was funded by Atlantic. Bert Berns, who oversaw Bang Records, was a prominent figure in the early 1960s music industry. He had an excellent track record of discovering talent, having worked with Solomon Burke and Wilson Pickett, and written songs for the Drifters. In England, he produced the Rock group 'Them,' for whom he wrote the hit song 'Here Comes The Night.' The band's lead singer was an unknown artist named Van Morrison, who was also signed to Bang Records. With all these elements in place, Neil Diamond was poised for his big break, and this time, he was fully prepared for success.

Among the songs that he wrote during this period were "Cherry, Cherry" and "Solitary Man". "Solitary Man" was the first record that Diamond recorded under his own name that made the charts. It remains one of his personal favorites, as it was about his early years as a songwriter, even though he failed to realize it at the time. He describes the song as "an outgrowth of my despair".
Diamond's breakthrough as a songwriter came in November 1965 with "Sunday and Me", a Top 20

hit for Jay and the Americans. Greater success followed with "I'm a Believer", "A Little Bit Me, a Little Bit You", "Look Out (Here Comes Tomorrow)", and "Love to Love", all performed by the Monkees. He wrote and recorded the songs for himself, but the cover versions were released before his own.

This hit song didn't just open doors for him; it completely obliterated them, propelling him to new heights of fame.. After the success of 'Cherry Cherry', Don Kirschner, the producer of the self-titled TV show "The Monkees," contacted Neil and asked if he had any similar songs. Neil sold him the rights to four songs, including 'I'm A Believer', which went on to become a massive hit. The single was released in 1966, hit #1 on Billboard's Hot 100 in January 1967, and remained there for seven consecutive weeks. It sold more than five million copies in the United States alone, surpassing the Beatles' 'Penny Lane' and the Rolling Stones' 'Ruby Tuesday.' Neil had been working hard to write a hit for a long time, and his perseverance and talent were finally rewarded.

As 'I'm A Believer' climbed the charts, Neil continued to perform at various venues, including Fred Weintraub's Bitter End club in Greenwich Village and Dave Hull's Hullabaloo club on Sunset Strip in Florida. He played as many clubs as possible to perfect his stage presence, which paid off in the long run. He was invited to perform at The Hollywood Bowl and the Cow Palace, armed with a strong repertoire of hits, and his stage persona was that of a brooding loner dressed in all black, similar to Johnny Cash. By the end of the decade, Neil Diamond had become a recognized star with a sizable following and favorable reviews.

The 1960s were not just a time of professional growth for Neil Diamond; it was also a time of social and cultural upheaval. The civil rights movement was gaining momentum, and the Vietnam War was dividing the nation. Diamond was no stranger to social and political activism, and he used his platform to express his views on these issues.

Diamond became increasingly frustrated with Bang Records as he desired to produce more profound, reflective music, exemplified by his 1968 hit "Brooklyn Roads." However, Bang's owner, Bert Berns, preferred "Kentucky Woman" as a single. Diamond no longer wished to write simplistic pop songs and instead proposed "Shilo," a tune about an imaginary childhood friend.

Despite Diamond's passion for the track, Bang deemed it not commercially viable, relegating it to an LP track on the album "Just for You." Along with his dissatisfaction over his royalties, Diamond attempted to leave Bang Records by utilizing a loophole in his contract that did not bind him exclusively to either WEB IV or Tallyrand. Unfortunately, the result was a sequence of legal

battles that coincided with a decline in his record sales and career prospects.

Although a magistrate denied WEB IV's request for a temporary injunction to prevent Diamond from signing with another record company while his contract dispute continued in court, the lawsuits persisted until February 1977. Diamond ultimately emerged victorious, securing the rights to his Bang-era master tapes.

In 1969, Diamond released the album "Brother Love's Travelling Salvation Show," which featured the hit single "Sweet Caroline." While the song is now a beloved classic, its origin was actually inspired by Caroline Kennedy, the daughter of President John F. Kennedy. Diamond was captivated by a photo of Caroline riding a horse, and he began writing the song about her. However, the song's lyrics became more abstract as he worked on it, and it ultimately became a tribute to the enduring spirit of hope and optimism.

The 1960s also saw Diamond become involved in various social causes.

In 1968, he performed at a benefit concert for the Student Nonviolent Coordinating Committee, a civil rights organization. He also performed at a concert in support of the United Farm Workers in

1970, and he was an active supporter of the anti-apartheid movement in South Africa.

From then onwards, Neil Diamond entered a prolific period, cementing his status as a great songwriter. However, he was keenly aware that he needed to progress and evolve his style to match his contemporaries such as Bob Dylan, Paul Simon, and Joni Mitchell.

Neil had to move away from the "Bubblegum" pop that had been his trademark sound in the early to mid-sixties, and by the end of the decade, he seemed to have accomplished this. He penned hits such as "Sweet Caroline" and "Holly Holy" in 1969, as well as other songs that showcased a more mature writing style, including "And The Grass Won't Pay No Mind," "Brooklyn Roads," and "And The Singer Sings His Song." These compositions were more profound and meaningful than his earlier pop tunes, reflecting Neil's desire to be viewed as a serious artist and a major force in the contemporary music scene.

In 1969, Neil Diamond relocated to Los Angeles, hoping to expand his songwriting horizons and immerse himself in the heart of the contemporary music scene.

The 1970s would prove to be the decade that so-lidified Neil Diamond's status as the world's pre-mier recording artist and songwriter.

The 1970´s: Studio Artist and Live Icon

Neil Diamond began the 1970s on the right path with his first #1 hit single, 'Crackling Rosie', a catchy pop tune featuring the repetitive chant "Play it now, play it now, play it now, my baby". This followed the success of his previous hit, 'Sweet Caroline', released the year before. In 1970, Diamond embarked on a project to create a concept album based on the music of Africa, titled 'Tap Root Manuscript'. This was a daring move that had his record label initially uncertain, but it proved successful, spawning multiple top forty hits and another #1 single in 'Crackling Rosie'.

For Diamond, 1970 was a critical year as he sought to prove his worth to his new label Uni, following a battle with his former label Bang Records over the release of 'Shilo'. Diamond's performances at the Troubadour, a prestigious venue for musicians, were also recorded and released as a live album titled 'GOLD'. These performances showcased his honed stagecraft, highlighting his growth as an artist.

Also his musical style underwent a significant

shift. He began to incorporate more introspective and personal lyrics into his songs, and he also experimented with a more mellow sound that was less reliant on the driving rhythms and hooks of his early work.

"Cracklin' Rosie" and "Song Sung Blue" were prime examples of this new sound. Both songs featured simple, memorable melodies and sing-along choruses that were easy for audiences to latch onto. They were also notable for their more subdued instrumentation, which relied on acoustic guitars and gentle percussion.

"Sweet Caroline" was another key song in this transitional period for Diamond. While it still had the sing-along chorus that had become a hallmark of his music, it also featured more a more polished production that showcased Diamond's evolving songwriting skills.

The release of "I Am...I Said" in 1971 marked Diamond's most intensely personal effort to date. The

song was a Top 5 hit in both the US and UK and took over four months to complete.

Neil was not content to rest on his achievements, and so he spent the first half of 1972 in the recording studio, working on a new album titled 'Moods'. The album was released in July of that year and included the hit single 'Song Sung Blue', which topped the charts. Other tracks on the album, such as 'Play Me' and 'Walk On Water', also became popular and helped establish Neil as a serious adult performer. 'Moods' was Neil's most successful album to date, and it marked the end of his con-

tract with Uni and MCA. He had one more album to produce for them, and he decided to record it at the Greek Theatre, his favorite venue, in August of that year.

During preparations for the concerts, Neil received offers for a new contract from three companies: MCA, Warner Bros, and Columbia, run by the influential Clive Davis. Recognizing Neil's track record of eight consecutive Gold albums, Davis made him an unprecedented offer: a five-year contract for five albums, each worth one million dollars. Neil accepted the offer and signed with Columbia.

Neil poured his energy into his Greek Theatre performances, incorporating songs from 'Moods' and using more instruments and a quadraphonic sound system to surpass his previous year's shows. The sold-out concerts were a resounding success, with Robert Hilburn of the Los Angeles Times declaring them "More of a triumph in every measurable way than his stunning shows last summer." The resulting live album, 'Hot August Night', soared to the top of the charts and remained a top seller until 1974, outperforming any other Diamond album. In fact, the album was still in the Australian top ten in 1976.

Following the success of Hot August Night, Diamond continued to tour extensively, playing to sold-out crowds around the world. In the fall of 1972, he performed for 20 consecutive nights at the Winter Garden Theater in New York City, becoming the first rock-era star to headline on Broadway. His concerts became known for their elaborate staging, including pyrotechnics, elaborate lighting, and backup dancers.

Diamond's live performances were also notable for his connection with his fans. He would often speak directly to the audience, sharing stories about his life and the inspiration behind his music. He would encourage fans to sing along with his hits and even invited some fans onto the stage to dance with him. Diamond's concerts became events, with fans traveling from around the world to see him perform.

Seclusion, Sabbatical and Seagulls

After a flawless performance at the Winter Garden, Neil Diamond left the stage to wild cheers from the audience, knowing it would be a long time before he returned.

Feeling exhausted after six long years on the road, Neil Diamond decided to take a seclusion, which would allow him to spend quality time with his family, especially his two-year-old son. He wanted to bond with him and build a fatherly relationship since he believed that his son needed him more than his audiences. During his sabbatical, Neil planned to rediscover himself, to get a clear understanding of who he was as a person, apart from the public perception, reviewers, record companies, and the industry in general. He said, "I wanted to regain a sense of who Neil Diamond was."

Before Neil could fully enjoy his temporary retirement, he had one more significant project to complete. Hall Bartlett, the film director working on the motion picture of the famous novel 'Jonathan Livingston Seagull,' approached Neil immediately after his Winter Garden performances, asking him to write the score for the movie.

This project would also become Neil's first album for his new employer, Columbia. The soundtrack album was released in October 1973 and became an overwhelming success even before the movie's release, reaching number 2 on the album chart.

It eventually became the highest-grossing soundtrack in history until it was surpassed by the score of 'Saturday Night Fever' in 1978.

To date, Jonathan Livingston Seagull remains Neil's best-selling album in America Diamond won both a Golden Globe Award for Best Original Score and a Grammy Award for Best Score Soundtrack Album for a Motion Picture for his work on the soundtrack.

In the aftermath, Neil said of the experience with Jonathan -

"It took one whole year of my life, and I honestly don't know what it took out of me, it probably gave me more than it took, but it was the hardest year of my life."

Diamond's career also had some controversies during this time. He and Richard Bach, author of Jonathan Livingston Seagull, both sued Hall Bartlett over the film adaptation. Bach disowned the film because he felt it omitted too much from the original novella, while Diamond felt that the film had butchered his score.

Bartlett responded angrily to the lawsuit, criticizing Diamond's music as "too slick" and stating that his arrogance was just a cover for his lonely and insecure nature.

Serenade

In 1974, Neil Diamond released his album "Serenade" under Columbia Records. The album was produced by Tom Catalano and was recorded at the Record Plant in Los Angeles. "Serenade" included hits such as "Longfellow Serenade" and "I've Been This Way Before," which were also released as singles.

The album was greatly influenced by the romantic writers that had captivated Neil's imagination during his youth, particularly evident in the lyrics of the song 'Longfellow Serenade'. Despite receiving mixed reviews from critics, the album was embraced by his fanbase and debuted directly in the top ten.

The lead single, 'Longfellow Serenade', achieved commercial success, peaking at number five on the charts.

"I've Been This Way Before" was originally intended to be a part of the Jonathan Livingston Seagull film score, but Diamond completed it too late for inclusion in the film. The song is a reflective piece that explores the cyclical nature of life and change. It became a hit on its own, reaching number 34 on the Billboard Hot 100 chart.

In the same year, Diamond also made a guest appearance on a TV special for the famous Welsh singer Shirley Bassey. During the show, Diamond performed a duet with Bassey, which showcased the pair's chemistry and vocal talents.

It was a very prominent appearance, and probably sated Neil's desire to perform, despite being on a touring break.

Beautiful Noise

Neil Diamond brought about several changes in his career, including setting up an office on Melrose Place in west Hollywood and employing a new manager, Fred Weintraub. Weintraub was a well-connected man in the industry and had organized concerts for many of popular music's biggest stars. This appointment was followed by Neil enlisting the services of Robbie Robertson, a fellow Californian neighbor, for his next album.

Robertson, known for writing hits like 'The Night They Drove Old Dixie Down' and 'The Weight,' was a member of the rock group 'The Band' and had become friends with Neil after they met in 1975. Their collaboration led to the creation of Neil's album 'Beautiful Noise,' which was a concept album based on his years as a struggling musician in New York's "Tin Pan Alley."

The album was well-received by critics and fans alike. The album's title track, "Beautiful Noise," opens the record with a stomping beat and a soaring chorus that exemplifies Diamond's knack for crafting catchy hooks. The song's lyr-

ics describe the power of music to uplift and inspire, a theme that runs throughout the album. Diamond's vocals are at their most emotive and expressive, soaring over the driving rhythm section and swirling guitars.

Beautiful Noise was a commercial and critical success upon its release, reaching No. 4 on the Billboard 200 chart and earning Diamond a Grammy nomination for Best Male Pop Vocal Performance. The album's blend of rock, pop, and folk influenc-

es, along with Diamond's impeccable songwriting and passionate vocals, have ensured its enduring popularity and continued relevance to this day. While Neil continued working on songs for the album, he also planned for the next chapter in his career - a return to the stage.

Return To The Stage

Neil started with an Australian tour called "The 'Thank You Australia' Concert", which was broadcast on 36 television outlets nationwide.

Later that year, Diamond returned to the United States to perform a series of shows at the Greek Theater in Los Angeles.

Neil Diamond challenged himself once again returning to the iconic "Greek Theatre" in Los Angeles.

Given his legendary early successes at the venue, it was natural for Diamond to feel a level of unease going into these performances. He pondered how he could present something different that could surpass the expectations of his audience.

Gone were the "Rock and Roll" elements of his previous appearances. Instead, Neil dazzled his fans with his bejewelled, stylish, and sophisticated look, every inch the superstar he had always aspired to be and had finally become.

Neil's music had matured, and so had he. His fans were not disappointed, and the shows were a re-sounding triumph.

The concerts were recorded and released as the live album "Love at the Greek," which featured a number of guest appearances, including duets with Helen Reddy and Henry Winkler (aka Arthur "The Fonz" Fonzarelli from "Happy Days").

During this time, Diamond began wearing colorful beaded shirts on stage, designed and made by Bill Whitten, to ensure that everyone in the audience could see him without binoculars.

Previously Neil had turned down various offers to play in Las Vegas again. However, he received an offer he couldn't refuse - to become the first per-former to play at Las Vegas' newly built Aladdin Hotel Theatre.

He accepted the deal and performed three con-certs, earning him $500,000, the highest payment for a Vegas performer at the time, even surpassing Frank Sinatra.

The show played to sold-out crowds and drew a "who's who" of Hollywood on opening night, with everyone from Elizabeth Taylor to Chevy Chase in attendance.

Diamond walked out on stage to a standing ovation and opened the show with a story about an ex-girlfriend who had dumped him before he became successful.

His lead-in line to the first song of the evening was, "You may have dumped me a bit too soon, baby, because look who's standing here tonight."

The Vegas shows were a great success, adding another first for Neil Diamond. The combination of his successful album and his triumphant return to the stage set the stage for a new era in Neil Diamond's career.

Neil also made arrangements for a summer European tour, playing historic venues such as Woburn Abbey and the London Palladium in front of Princess Margaret. The European tour was filmed by William Friedkin, but the project was scrapped due to sound quality issues.

However, Neil and TV director Art Fisher salvaged usable footage to create a TV documentary entitled 'I'm Glad You're Here With Me Tonight'.

The album of the same name went platinum, and a particular song from the album – 'You Don't Bring Me Flowers' – became a pop standard after a successful duet with Barbra Streisand that went to number one on the charts.

After scrapping his initial project of cover versions titled "The American Popular Song," Neil's employers at Columbia convinced him to take advantage of the popularity of his hit "You Don't Bring me Flowers." The success of the song became the title of his next album, which was released in November 1978 and rose to number four on the charts, becoming one of Diamond's best-sellers. The album also featured another well-known hit: "Forever In Blue Jeans."

In early 1979, Neil had to cut short a concert tour due to the birth of his son, and he considered his kids to be his greatest achievements, even better than his best songs and performances.

He resumed the tour but then collapsed on stage. Doctors found a tumor on his spine, which required a 12-hour operation to remove. He had been losing feeling in his right leg for a number of years but had ignored it. When he collapsed, he had no strength in either leg. Diamond was so convinced he was going to die that he wrote farewell letters to his friends.

However the tumor was successfully removed, and by June of that year, Neil was back on his feet. He resumed touring at the same venue where he

collapsed, the "Cow Palace," and worked on a new album of original material and covers of other songs called "September Morn," which went platinum.

However, his focus shifted when he was approached to star in a motion picture, a modern update of the Al Jolson classic "The Jazz Singer".

The Jazz-Singer

In the 1980s, Neil Diamond had a tumultuous relationship with Hollywood.
He was offered the lead role in a planned film version of "You Don't Bring Me Flowers" alongside Barbra Streisand, but the project fell through.
Instead, Diamond decided to star in a remake of the Al Jolson classic, The Jazz Singer.

Neil Diamond took on the massive responsibility of starring in the film and composing the soundtrack, which was no small feat.

Despite having no prior acting experience, he received a whopping upfront guarantee of four million dollars for his work, the largest for any actor at the time. Neil was anxious about the genuineness of his on-screen performances, and thus he insisted on being captured singing "live" instead of mouthing along to a pre-recorded backing track.

Moreover, he was apprehensive about co-starring with Laurence Olivier, often regarded as one of the greatest screen actors of all time.
This made Neil consult with another acting icon, Dustin Hoffman, who advised him to act as nat-

urally as possible and take any additional advice.

"The Jazz Singer" depicts the story of Yussel Rabinowitz, the son of a Jewish cantor (played by Neil Diamond) who defies his orthodox father's (played by Olivier) wishes and pursues his dream of rock superstardom, breaking from the tradition of a Rabinowitz serving as a Cantor at the Synagogue. Although the album went gold and included three hit singles, namely "Love On the Rocks," "Hello Again," and "America," the film received mixed reviews.

"America" was a tribute to Diamond's grandparents, who were immigrants, and the song resonated with many people who identified with the immigrant experience. It became an anthem for many important events, including the return of hostages from Iran, the 100th anniversary of the Statue of Liberty, and a tribute to Martin Luther King Jr.

Despite the success of the soundtrack, the film itself was a failure. Diamond had never acted professionally before and found it challenging to handle the demands of the role. He even won a Razzie Award for Worst Actor, although he was also nominated for a Golden Globe Award for the same role.

Despite this setback, Diamond was proud of the film and saw it as a "bar mitzvah" moment, where he was finally able to embrace and celebrate his Jewish heritage.

However, Neil faced severe criticism from some reviewers, with one stating that he had accomplished nothing and that he had only played himself. Neil took the negative comments in stride, as he believed that he had shared a slice of Jewish culture with the masses.

The 1980s did not begin on a positive note for Neil due to his unpleasant experience with "The Jazz Singer." Despite putting his all into the role and having genuine ambitions of pursuing an acting career, the ordeal turned him away from that sector of the entertainment industry.

Crossroads

In the 80ies Neil Diamond found himself at a critical juncture in his profession, having veered away from his earlier Rock & Roll origins, both as a composer and performer, while the latest music trends like "Punk" and "New Wave" dominated the headlines. Nevertheless, Columbia Records believed that Neil still had a strong appeal and offered him an eight-album deal worth $30 million.

Under this agreement, Neil's first album was 'On the Way to the Sky', which produced three hit singles - the title track, 'On the Way to the Sky,' 'Be Mine Tonight,' and 'Yesterday's Songs,' and became an enormous success, selling over 1.5 million copies within six months. Columbia's investment in Neil appeared to be a great bargain.

From 1981 to 1982, Neil Diamond traveled the United States, playing to packed audiences. During one of his days off, he, along with his wife Marcia and their showbiz friends and fellow songwriters Burt Bacharach and Carol Bayer-Sager, watched a screening of "E.T. - The

Extraterrestrial" in a cinema. The film's storyline inspired the trio so much that they composed their most well-known collaboration, 'Heartlight.'
The single climbed to number five on the charts, becoming Neil's highest-selling single since 'America' from 'The Jazz Singer.'

The album 'Heartlight' was released in 1982. Although the song never mentions the film's title character, Universal Pictures, which had released E.T. and was the parent company of the Uni Records label (by then called MCA Records), briefly threatened legal action against Diamond and Columbia Records. 2. Although the song never mentions the film's title character, Universal Pictures, which had released E.T. and was the parent company of the Uni Records label (by then called MCA Records), briefly threatened legal action against Diamond and Columbia Records.

Neil Diamond spent the rest of 1982 and the beginning of 1983 on tour and writing music. In March 1983, Neil was honored with induction into the Songwriter's Hall Of Fame in New York City, alongside Sammy Cahn, Fred Ebb, and John Kander. This was a fitting acknowledgment of Neil's long-lasting career and songwriting abilities, as he was included with such esteemed figures.

June 13, 1983, was declared Neil Diamond Day in Los Angeles, with radio stations playing his hits in anticipation of his opening night at the Forum. Nearly 130,000 people saw Neil perform over the seven-night residency, breaking the venue's revenue and attendance records previously held by Elton John. Neil had planned to tape the concerts for another "Live" album, but he strangely chose not to follow through with the album.

Neil focused on working on a new studio album, 'Primitive,' his third in as many years, following 'On the Way to the Sky' and 'Heartlight.' However, little did Neil know that this album would cause a significant rift in his relationship with Columbia Records. The executives at Columbia didn't believe that 'Primitive' was Neil's best work. According to an insider, Diamond vehemently disagreed, and on March 1, 1984, he filed a lawsuit in Santa Monica, California, to order the company to release the record.

In 1984, Neil Diamond continued his concert tours and began the process of creating a new album as part of his contract with Columbia Records. He initially titled the album 'Story of my Life,' but upon completion, Columbia was once again unhappy with the result. Neil then set out to rework the album under a new title, 'Headed For The Future.' He was determined to make it a success and enlisted the help of some of the biggest names in the music industry, including David Foster, Stevie Wonder, and Maurice White of Earth Wind and Fire.

The album peaked at number 20 on the Billboard 200 chart. While it didn't have the same success as some of his earlier albums, it still showed that he was dedicated to creating new music and trying to adapt to changing musical tastes.

Around this same time, Diamond made a return to television with his first special in nine years, Hello Again. The special featured a mix of comedy sketches and musical performances, including a duo medley with Carol Burnett. This appearance helped to keep Diamond in the public eye and maintain his fan base.

In 1987, Diamond had the honor of singing the national anthem at the Super Bowl, which was a huge platform for him to showcase his talents to a massive audience. He continued to show his patriotic side by having his song "America" become the theme song for Michael Dukakis' 1988 presidential campaign. Despite the lack of chart suc-

cess, Diamond was still able to have his music reach a wide audience through other avenues.

In 1988, Neil Diamond collaborated with David Foster once again to produce his latest album, 'The Best Years Of Our Lives'. Foster's reputation as a top-notch producer made him highly sought after. As was customary throughout the decade, Diamond planned yet another World Tour.

This new tour took Diamond back to Europe and England, where he hadn't performed in five years. During his last performance in Britain, he had even performed in front of the British Royalty. Although his record sales were dwindling, Diamond was still considered one of the most popular concert draws in the music industry. This was the driving force behind his unyielding love for performing.

Neil Diamond was the top performer in terms of box office sales on the concert circuit, his concert tour ended on November 22, 1989 and conclued a decade that had its share of highs and also lows.

New Headaches

Despite facing upheavals in the past, the new decade brought fresh concerns for the accomplished artist. With evolving music trends, Diamond's primary worry was whether he would continue to be relevant, both as a recording artist and a performer, despite his previous successes.

Neil Diamond's popularity continued to soar throughout the 1990s, with his hit song "Sweet Caroline" becoming an anthem for sports fans across the United States. Originally released back in 1969, the song's upbeat melody and catchy chorus made it the perfect sing-along song for fans at sporting events. Its popularity grew particularly strong among Boston sports teams, with the Boston Red Sox and Boston College football and basketball teams regularly playing the song during their games.

The song's popularity even extended beyond the United States, with it being played at sporting events in other countries, such as a rugby tournament in Hong Kong and a soccer match in Northern Ireland. The song became so ubiquitous at sporting events that it eventually became the theme song of "Red Sox Nation," the nickname given to fans of the Boston Red Sox. The New York Rangers also adapted it as their own, playing it whenever they were winning at the end of the third period of their games. The Pittsburgh Panthers football team played it after the third quarter of all home games, with the crowd cheering, "Let's go Pitt." The Carolina Panthers played it at the end of every home game they won, and the Davidson College pep band played it in the second half of every Davidson Wildcats men's basketball home game.

Despite his success with "Sweet Caroline," Diamond remained active in producing new music throughout the 1990s. In fact, he released six studio albums during the decade, including covers of classic songs from movies and famous Brill Building-era songwriters. He also released two Christmas albums, one of which peaked at No. 8 on Billboard's Album chart.

In addition to producing new music, Diamond also continued to perform at live events throughout the 1990s. In 1992, he performed for President George H. W. Bush's final Christmas in Washington NBC special, and in 1993 he opened the Mark of the Quad Cities (now the iWireless Center) with two shows to a crowd of over 27,000 people.

In 1994, Neil Diamond faced one of the most difficult challenges in his personal life: the end of his marriage to Marcia Murphey. The couple had been married for 25 years, and their divorce was a shock to many fans and friends. Diamond and Murphey had met in the mid-1960s, when she was working as a production assistant for a TV show in Los Angeles. They got married in 1969 and had two children together.

Despite their long and seemingly happy marriage, rumors of trouble had been swirling around the couple for years before their divorce. Diamond was known for his busy touring schedule, which kept him away from home for long periods of time. He also struggled with depression and other personal issues, which put a strain on the marriage.

When news of the divorce broke, Diamond issued a statement saying that he and Marcia had "grown apart" and that they would "remain the best of friends."

Neil offered Marcia a divorce settlement of $150 million, affirming that she deserved every penny. This remains one of the largest divorce payouts in the history of the entertainment industry.

The end of his marriage was a difficult period for Diamond, but he continued to focus on his music and career. In 1996, he released the album "Tennessee Moon," which included collaborations with a number of prominent country artists as Waylon Jennings, and Buffy Lawson.

The album marked a departure from Diamond's typical sound, incorporating more twangy guitar and fiddle arrangements. The album also included "Kentucky Woman," a re-recording of Diamond's 1967 hit song.

"Tennessee Moon" was well-received by both fans and critics, with many praising Diamond's foray into country music. The album reached No. 3 on the US Country chart and was certified gold by the RIAA. Diamond supported the album with a tour.

Its also worth mentioning, that various films were incorporating Neil Diamond's songs into their soundtracks. The grunge band Urge Overkill performed "Girl You'll Be A Woman Soon," originally a mega-hit by Neil Diamond, in the movie "Pulp Fiction." "Love On the Rocks" was featured in the Al Pacino and Johnny Depp movie "Donnie Brasco," while "Sweet Caroline" was used in the Matt Damon film "Beautiful Girls."

It seemed that even as the late 1990s approached,

Neil Diamond's music remained relevant and sought after as the ideal addition to a movie soundtrack.

Neil Diamond's love for the cinema was no secret, and it was only fitting that his songs were being featured in various movies. With this passion in mind, he embarked on his next project, an album simply titled 'The Movie Album', which would include some of the most iconic songs from films. The album would pay tribute to classics like 'Moon River' from Breakfast at Tiffany's, starring Audrey Hepburn, and 'Secret Love', from Calamity Jane, a Doris Day classic. It would also feature a tribute to Frank Sinatra, who had recently passed away. For the recording of this album, Diamond opted for a full "Live" orchestra, with the legendary Elmer Bernstein conducting.

Following the completion of 'The Movie Album', Diamond hit the road again for another tour. By the end of the 1998-1999 tour, he was declared the top solo touring artist of the 1990s by Amusement Business Magazine. This was a remarkable feat considering that he did not have a single top ten hit throughout the entire decade.

Floodgates Opened

The entertainment industry's fixation on Neil Diamond persisted in 2001. The California-based rock group "Smashmouth" recorded a rendition of 'I'm A Believer' for the score of the animated hit 'Shrek,' and it soared to the top spot on the charts. Diamond reciprocated by composing 'You Are My Number One' for the band's ensuing album. Additionally, he played a more prominent role in the 2001 madcap comedy 'Saving Silverman,' which had a Neil Diamond tribute band known as "Diamonds in the Rough." The film, which was titled 'Evil Woman' outside North America, chronicled how one of the members' girlfriends coerced him into abandoning the band and destroying all of his Diamond records and memorabilia. Neil Diamond appeared in the film as himself, opposite Jack Black, Steve Zahn, Jason Biggs, Amanda Peet, and R. Lee Ermey, who made a guest appearance and gained notoriety for his role in 'Full Metal Jacket.'

Neil wrote a few tracks for the film, which opened a creative floodgate for him. ""It was like I had opened up a faucet inside me," he explained. As a result, he continued writing, which led to the genesis of an album. 'Three Chord Opera' was more than just any album; it was Diamond's first project since 'Serenade' in 1974, in which he wrote all of the songs himself. It was also his first album of original material since 'Lovescape' in 1991. The fans were ecstatic, and the album debuted at number five on the charts, marking the highest opening week performance of Diamond's career to date.

In 2005, Neil Diamond released his critically acclaimed album "12 Songs", produced by Rick Rubin. This album marked a departure from his usual sound, as it was a more stripped-down and basic approach to his music. It was released in two versions, a standard 12-song release, and a special edition with two bonus tracks, one of which featured backing vocals by Brian Wilson. The album debuted at No. 4 on the Billboard chart, and it received mostly positive reviews, with many critics considering it as one of Diamond's best sets of songs in a long time.

In 2007, Neil Diamond embarked on his second collaboration with Rick Rubin, commencing the writing of new songs.

There was no cause for concern that Columbia records would mishandle Diamond's upcoming album, as he had established valuable connections in high positions. Rubin had ascended to co-leadership of Columbia records and had won the Grammy award for producer of the year in 2007. Diamond devoted a year to crafting his new album, titled 'Home before Dark.'

Diamond revealed that he felt quite solitary during the songwriting process for 'Home Before Dark,' mostly due to the struggles his then-girlfriend Rachel Farley was facing with a spinal condition. Despite this, the situation helped Diamond tap into his emotions and bring forth his best work on an emotional level.

The album reached number one on the album chart, giving Neil his first ever number one album.

In 2007, Neil Diamond was also inducted into the Long Island Music Hall of Fame.

In 2008, Diamond appeared as a guest mentor on the television show American Idol, where the contestants sang his songs. During the show's broadcast, he premiered a new song, "Pretty Amazing Grace," from his then-recently-released album "Home Before Dark."

The album was released on May 6, 2008, and it topped the charts in New Zealand, the United Kingdom, and the United States.

In June 2008, Diamond played to an estimated 108,000 fans at the Glastonbury Festival in Somerset, England, as part of his Concert of a Lifetime Tour. However, technical problems marred the concert. In August of the same year, Diamond allowed cameras to record his entire four-night run at New York's Madison Square Garden, which he released as a DVD in the US in 2009.

On February 6, 2009, Neil Diamond was honored as the MusiCares Person of the Year, two nights before the 51st Annual Grammy Awards.

In July of the same year, Diamond was invited to sing at the Independence Day celebration in Boston, where he performed his hit song "Sweet Caroline."
On October 13, 2009, he released "A Cherry Cherry Christmas," his third album of Christmas music.

Legacy

In 2010, Neil Diamond released his album "Dreams", which consisted of his favorite songs by rock-era artists, as well as a new version of his hit song "I'm a Believer." He appeared on NBC's The Sing-Off to perform a track from the album, "Ain't No Sunshine", alongside two a cappella groups. The album was well-received, and it marked a new era of Neil Diamond's career.

The following years, in 2011 and 2012, Diamond was inducted into the Rock and Roll Hall of Fame and received a lifetime achievement award from the Kennedy Center. He also received a star on the Hollywood Walk of Fame, and he topped the bill at the Royal Variety Performance in the UK. These honors cemented Diamond's place in music history as one of the most significant songwriters and performers of his generation.

In 2013, Diamond made an unannounced appearance at Fenway Park to perform "Sweet Caroline" during the 8th inning of the first game at Fenway since the Boston Marathon bombing. He also released the single "Freedom Song (They'll

Never Take Us Down)" to benefit the One Fund Boston and the Wounded Warrior Project. Diamond's performance on the west lawn of the U.S. Capitol as part of A Capitol Fourth was broadcast nationally by PBS on July 4, 2013.

In 2014, Diamond signed with the Capitol Music Group unit of Universal Music Group, which also owned Diamond's Uni/MCA catalog. His next album, "Melody Road", produced by Don Was and Jacknife Lee, was released in October 2014. Diamond surprised fans with a concert at his alma mater, Erasmus High School in Brooklyn, and announced a 2015 "Melody Road" World Tour, which used new media platforms and social media extensively.

In October 2016, Diamond released "Acoustic Christmas", a folk-inspired Christmas album that included original songs and acoustic versions of holiday classics. In March 2017, the career-spanning anthology "Neil Diamond 50 – 50th Anniversary Collection" was released. He began his final concert tour, the "50 Year Anniversary World Tour", in Fresno, California, in April. This tour was highly anticipated, and fans around the world eagerly awaited Diamond's arrival in their cities.

However, in January 2018, Diamond announced that he would be retiring from touring due to a diagnosis of Parkinson's disease. This announcement came as a shock to his fans, who were eagerly anticipating the final leg of his "50 Year Anniversary World Tour" in Australia and New Zealand. In a statement on his official website, Diamond assured fans that he was not retiring from music and that he would continue to write, record, and develop new projects.

Following his retirement from touring, Diamond kept a low profile and focused on his health. In July 2018, he made a surprise appearance at the Incident Command post in Basalt, Colorado, near his home, to thank firefighters and their families for their efforts in containing the Lake Christine Fire. He performed a solo acoustic guitar concert for the firefighters and their families as a gesture of gratitude for their hard work.

Although Diamond has not released any new music since his retirement from touring, his music continues to be celebrated by fans around the world. In 2019, his signature song "Sweet Caroline" was selected by the Library of Congress for preservation in the National Recording Registry for being "culturally, historically, or aesthetically significant."

Diamond's legacy as one of the greatest songwriters and performers of his generation remains firmly intact, and his music will continue to inspire generations of fans for years to come.

Broadway

The recently debuted jukebox musical "A Beautiful Noise" draws inspiration from the life and music of the renowned artist, Neil Diamond. The Broadway show premiered at the Broadhurst Theatre on December 4, 2022, and has been making waves ever since. According to reports, it generated more than $1 million in revenue in the week leading up to its premiere, which is a testament to its popularity among theater-goers.

The title of the musical, A Beautiful Noise, is derived from Diamond's 1976 album of the same name. The production was written by Anthony McCarten and produced by Ken Davenport and Bob Gaudio. The storyline revolves around a series of therapy sessions where Diamond responds to his lyrics as they are read to him by his psychiatrist from a second-hand copy of The Complete Lyrics of Neil Diamond.

In an interview with The Boston Globe in June 2022, McCarten explained that the therapist opens the book, and all of Diamond's 60 years of songwriting and exploration spill out into a magnificent musical collage. The songs, once unleashed from the book, take on lives of their own and carry the narrative forward.

The musical includes some of Neil Diamond's most iconic songs, including "Cracklin' Rosie," "Love on the Rocks," and "Sweet Caroline." These classic songs are performed with great energy and enthusiasm by the cast, making for a thoroughly enjoyable experience.

The lighting design is particularly impressive during the rendition of "Sweet Caroline," with blazing lights on stage turning night into day and causing the audience to rise from their seats and join in the singing and dancing.

Overall, the musical does justice to Diamond's legacy and is a must-watch for any fan of his music.

Part 2:

Captured Moments - A Visual Journey Through Memories

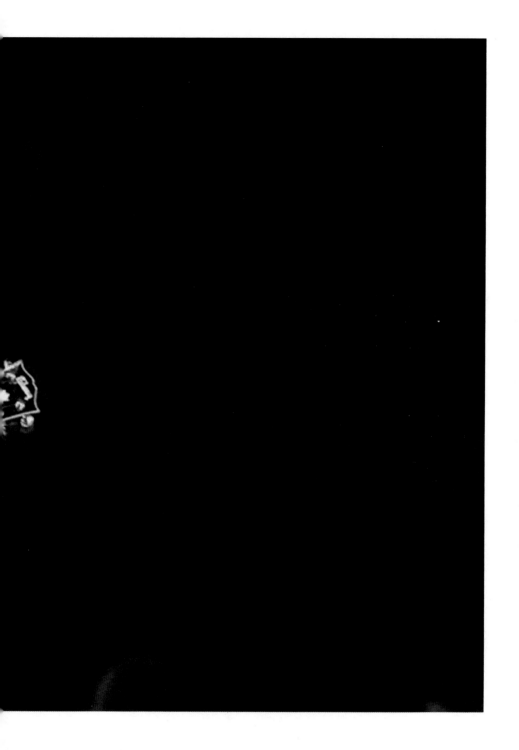

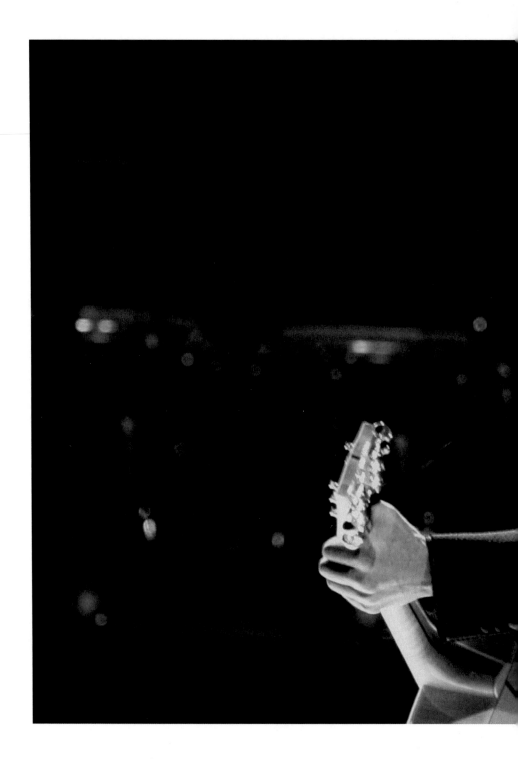

Alexander Gresbek

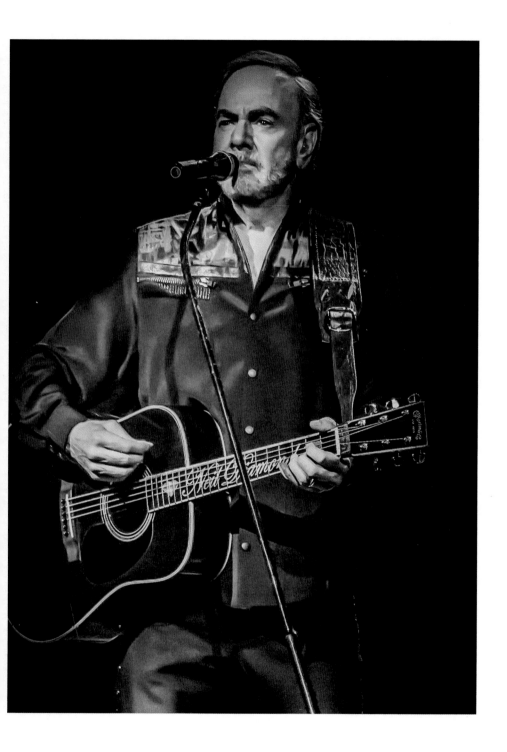

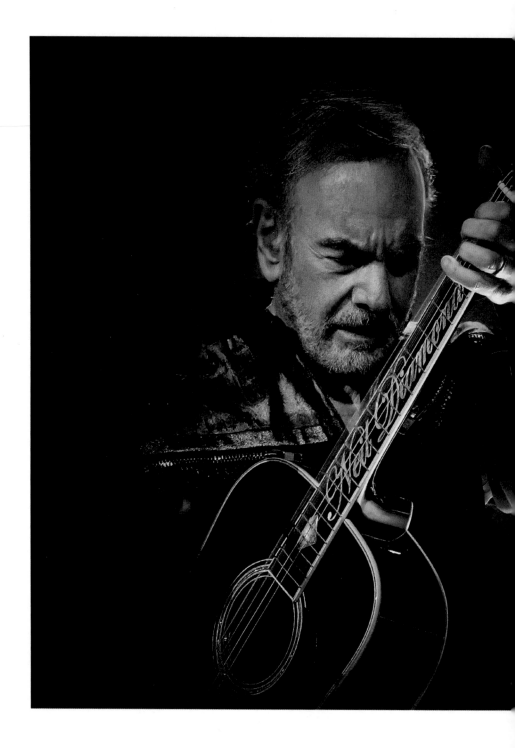

Alexander Gresbek

Part 3:
The Songwriter

Neil Diamond is widely known for his captivating live performances and velvety voice, drawing large crowds to arenas and stadiums worldwide. However, his roots lie in songwriting, which he has referred to as his true calling. Despite facing numerous rejections while trying to sell his earliest compositions, he persisted for eight long years until finally gaining recognition as a songwriter. This opened the floodgates, and Neil Diamond's catalogue now includes many timeless classics.

Unlike many singer-songwriters who emerged during the same era, such as the Beatles, Bob Dylan, and James Taylor, whose music spoke to the social and political issues of the time, Neil Diamond's songs have a spiritual element and a personal touch that is beautifully expressed through his eloquent lyrics. His themes often center around the deep sense of isolation and yearning for belonging and connection, balanced with a desire for freedom, and the ups and downs of love.

What sets Neil Diamond apart is his honesty and

simplicity in his songwriting, with a talent for making the most of just three chords. From his early bubblegum pop tunes to his later works with strong religious overtones, such as 'Holly Holy,' 'Canta Libre,' and 'Soolaimon,' Neil Diamond's songs speak to the whole range of human emotions and experiences, showcasing his unique insight into the human condition.

Beyond his natural genius and dedication to his craft, Neil Diamond's unapologetic emotional honesty and commitment to connecting with his audience make him a true gem in the music industry. He is a romantic at heart, much like the poets of the Renaissance, and this trait shines through his writing, revealing his deep connection to his art.

Despite his immense talents, Neil Diamond may still be underrated, and it's possible that he hasn't received the recognition he deserves as both a songwriter and a singer/performer. But for those who appreciate the beauty and sincerity in his music, he will always remain a timeless icon.

Part 4:
The Singer

It's a surprising fact in the music industry that Neil Diamond never received any formal training in singing. Despite this, he possesses one of the most identifiable and defining voices in music, with his smooth and rich delivery bringing his famous songs to life. It's even more surprising that Diamond never intended to pursue a career as a singer. Instead, his main aim was to become a songwriter, which he found more appealing. He never craved the spotlight, yet he took to singing effortlessly.

As a young artist struggling to sell his earliest compositions, Diamond turned to singing his own songs as a means to get them heard. This move paid off when he caught the attention of the husband-and-wife songwriting duo, Jeff Barry and Ellie Greenwich, launching his massively successful career.

Listening to Neil Diamond's music draws us in with the warmth and sincerity in his voice. There's a certain authenticity and truthfulness in his singing that isn't often heard in other artists. As Diamond had no formal training in music, he was free to convey his songs in his own way, making a strong connection with his listeners. This is what initially attracted me to his music - his voice gave his already fantastic songs a unique feeling and life of their own. Few artists can connect with their fans the way Neil Diamond does.

If Neil Diamond had solely worked as a writer and not a singer, would his songs have become as famous as they are today? Probably not. Not because his songs lack quality, but because Neil himself interprets them the way he intended when he wrote them. No other singer could do justice to his biggest hits, delivering them with the same style, emotion, feeling, truth, and sincerity that Neil Diamond does.

Diamond's voice fits his songs perfectly, creating an irresistible connection. The combination of his voice and his compositions makes his voice unique and he is the only one that should sing his songs.

Part 5: 50 Years

It is said that Neil Diamond is the "Marathon Man" of the music industry due to his longevity, outlasting many of his contemporaries. Neil Diamond's 50-year career in music is a testament to his talent, dedication, and staying power as an artist. From his early days as a Brill Building songwriter to his emergence as a solo artist in the late 1960s, Diamond has consistently delivered hits that have become beloved classics.

One of the things that sets Diamond apart from many of his peers is his ability to write songs that are both catchy and meaningful. Whether he's singing about love, loss, or the joys of life, his lyrics always seem to strike a chord with listeners. Songs like "Sweet Caroline," "Song Sung Blue," and "Forever in Blue Jeans" have become part of the fabric of popular culture, and are still played and sung by fans of all ages.

In addition to his songwriting prowess, Diamond is also an accomplished performer. His live shows are legendary, with audiences singing along to every word and cheering him on. His energy, charisma, and sheer joy of performing are infectious, and it's no wonder that he's still able to pack arenas and stadiums after all these years.

One of the things that makes Diamond's music so enduring is its timelessness. His songs speak to universal themes and emotions that never go out of style, and his melodies are catchy and memorable. But even as his music has remained a constant, Diamond himself has evolved and grown as an artist over the years. He's explored new genres and styles, collaborated with other artists, and continued to challenge himself creatively.

Of course, no reflection on Neil Diamond's 50-year career would be complete without mentioning his influence on other musicians. He's been covered by countless artists, and his songs have been used in movies, TV shows, and commercials. His impact on popular culture is undeniable, and his legacy as one of the greatest songwriters and performers of all time is secure.

In conclusion, Neil Diamond's 50-year career is a remarkable achievement that has brought joy, inspiration, and entertainment to millions of people around the world. His music is a testament to the power of songwriting and the enduring appeal of catchy melodies and heartfelt lyrics.

But beyond his talent as a musician and songwriter, Neil Diamond has also shown incredible resilience and perseverance throughout his career. He has faced numerous challenges, both personal and professional, and has always managed to come out on top, with his music and his spirit intact.

As I listen to his music today, I am reminded of the many milestones and memories of my own life that have been accompanied by the soundtrack of Neil Diamond's songs.

As a 12-year-old kid, I remember hearing "Beautiful Noise" on the radio for the very first time, and it immediately caught my attention. I went on to buy my first LP, which was none other than Neil Diamond's "Beautiful Noise," and that marked the beginning of my love for his music. Over time, I collected many of his other albums, each one adding to my appreciation of his songwriting, his unique voice, and his ability to capture a range of emotions in his music.

Listening to Neil Diamond's music became a part of my life, and his songs have been a constant source of comfort for me over the years.

I am grateful for the pleasure that his music has brought to me and to so many others, and I am filled with admiration for the man and his music.

So I want to close this reflection by saying thank you, Neil Diamond. Your music has brought joy, comfort, and inspiration to millions of people around the world for over 50 years.

Alexander Gresbek

Part 6:

Discographie

Studio albums:

- The Feel of Neil Diamond (1966)
- Just for You (1967)
- Velvet Gloves and Spit (1968)
- Brother Love's Travelling Salvation Show
- Touching You, Touching Me (1969)
- Tap Root Manuscript (1970)
- Stones (1971)
- Moods (1972)
- Jonathan Livingston Seagull (1973)
- Serenade (1974)
- Beautiful Noise (1976)
- I'm Glad You're Here with Me Tonight (1977)
- You Don't Bring Me Flowers (1978
- September Morn (1980)
- On the Way to the Sky (1981)
- Heartlight (1982)
- Primitive (1984)
- Headed for the Future (1986)
- The Best Years of Our Lives (1988)
- Lovescape (1991)
- The Christmas Album (1992)
- Up on the Roof: Songs from the Brill Building (1993)
- Tennessee Moon (1996)
- The Movie Album: As Time Goes By (1998)
- Three Chord Opera (2001)
- 12 Songs (2005)
- Home Before Dark (2008)
- Dreams (2010)
- Melody Road (2014)
- Classic Diamonds (2020)

Main Live albums:

- Gold: Recorded Live at the Troubadour (1970)
- Hot August Night (1972)
- Love at the Greek (1977)
- Hot August Night II (1987)
- Hot August Night/NYC (2009)

Compilation albums:

- Neil Diamond's Greatest Hits (no year)
- Gold Diamond (1972)
- Gold Diamond Volume 2 (1972)
- With Love from... Neil Diamond (1972)
- Diamonds (1974)
- World Hits (1974)
- Greatest Hits Vol. 2 (1974)
- Portrait (2 LPs) (1976)
- The Neil Diamond Show (3 LPs) (1977)
- Sweet Caroline (1978)
- 20 Diamond Hits (1979)
- Diamond Forever (1980)
- The Best of Neil Diamond (1980)
- Solid Gold (1980)
- Solitary Man (1981)
- Song Sung Blue (1982)
- The Best of Neil Diamond (UK: Gold) (1986)
- Greatest Hits (1986)
- Red, Red Wine (1988)
- Collection (1989)
- Classic (1989)

- The Collection (1991)
- Glory Road: 1968 to 1972 (1992)
- The Best Of (1992)
- The Best of Neil Diamond (1994)
- The Complete Bang Recordings (1994)
- Great Hits: The Originals (1995)
- The Neil Diamond Songbook (1995)
- The Neil Diamond Collection (1999)
- Play Me: The Complete UniStudio Recordings ... Plus! (3 CDs) (2002)
- The Very Best of Neil Diamond (2002)
- The Essential Collection (2004)
- Classics: The Early Years (2008)

Attribution / Sources:

All Images: Alexander Gresbek with the exeption of:

Pages 18, 22, 26, 30, 32, 41, 45: AI generated
Page 34: Public Domain (Wikipedia: Cardelús, Jen)
Pages 37, 38: Creative Commons (Wikipedia: Jessie Eastland)
Page 43: Creative Commons (Wikipedia: Skybird73)
Page 46: Creative Commons (Wikipedia: Jon Watts)
Page 54: Public Domain (Ronald Reagan Library Museum Collection (NAID 6816361)
Page 61: Fair Use
Page 71: Fair Use
Page 75: Public Domain (US Navy 090704-N-1928O-372 Mass Communication Specialist 3rd Class Anna Kiner, assigned to the USS Constitution)
Pages 76, 78: Creative Commons (Wikipedia: Eva Rinaldi)

Online sources:

https://en.wikipedia.org/wiki/Neil_Diamond
www.neildiamondcentral.com

Author

Alexander Gresbek

———

Born in 1965 in London, Alexander Gresbek completed his degree in business administration, specializing in marketing and foreign trade. He began his career as a logistics manager in Nuremberg, Düsseldorf and Bonn, where he gained valuable experience in international trade and supply chain management.

In 2018, Alexander and his wife Anuschka relocated to the Costa Blanca, where he now works as an author and photographer. His passion for photography began at a young age and has since grown into a career. Alexander's work has been published in various books, publications and online platforms.

As a life-long Neil Diamond fan, Alexander has combined his passion for photography with his love for music by taking pictures at Neil Diamond concerts he attended while living in Germany. The pictures in this book are a collection of some of his best shots, capturing the essence of Neil Diamond's performances and charisma as a performer.

Made in the USA
Las Vegas, NV
14 November 2024

cd3de5d4-f242-49c6-b753-5337e4f1f8f7R01